HUMAN BODY

Written by
Steve Pollock

Illustrated by
Salvatore Tomaselli and Claire Bushe

Edited by
Debbie Reid

Designed by
Jo Digby

Picture research by
Emma Segal

CONTENTS

Inside the human body

There are many systems in the human body which work to keep it going. They all work together and ensure that your body carries on working properly. These systems, which are all working inside you right now, will be covered in more detail in the rest of this book. They are:

The nervous system

The brain is the body's control centre, and messages are sent along nerves which are throughout the whole body.

The endocrine system

Special parts of your body release tiny amounts of chemicals called hormones that control your body chemistry.

The respiratory system

You need oxygen every minute of the day and night, and your lungs are working to keep you alive whether you are asleep or awake.

The skeletal system

Your skeleton protects the soft organs, supports your body and, along with the muscles, helps your body to move.

The excretory system

The kidneys are your waste filtering system. They get rid of most of the waste and pass it out in your urine which is stored in your bladder.

The muscular system

Without muscles, you could never move around. Besides moving the body around, muscles do many other jobs such as moving food along the gut and pumping blood around the body. But muscles can only pull, they never push.

The sensory system

Your senses help you stay in touch with the world. They allow you to experience new things which your brain can store and use in the future. Together, your sense organs and your brain help you learn about and understand the world you live in.

The circulatory system

Your heart pumps blood around your body through the vast network of blood vessels.

The digestive system

This breaks down the food you eat into chemicals which can pass into your body, and then removes any waste.

The reproductive system

These are the parts of the body, different in males and females, which allow us to make more humans.

The lymphatic system

This is the system which helps protect us from infections and diseases.

Find out how all these work as you go through the book.

Making sense of the world

What helps you to know what is going on around you? There are five different senses the human body can use to explore the world. These are: seeing, hearing, touching, tasting and smelling.

For humans to use these senses, a special part of the body is used. These are the sense organs: your eyes, ears, skin, tongue and nose.

Sense organs only collect information – they cannot make sense of it. They receive information and pass it on to the brain along your nervous system as electrical signals. As you grow older, the sense organs help you learn about the world. Each time something new happens, your brain stores the event so that you know what to do next time. All the sense organs are connected to the brain by nerves.

Think about the senses that you would use and what might happen when something rather tasty is cooking in the kitchen.

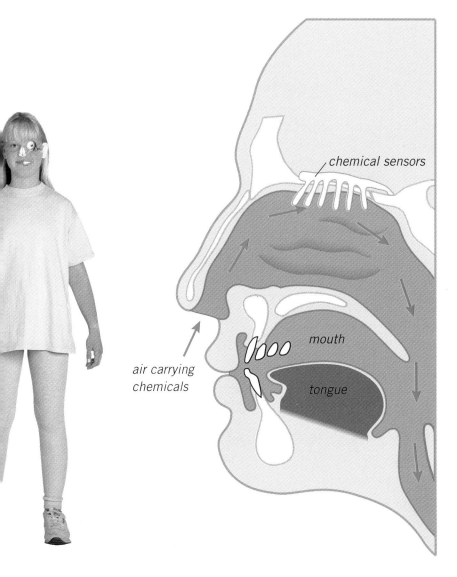

chemical sensors

air carrying chemicals

mouth

tongue

Smelling

Before you get to the kitchen, what sense is telling you that something is cooking? Heating up food releases chemicals as vapour which reach your nose. These stimulate the chemical sensors at the back of your nose, sending messages to your brain. After a time, the smell doesn't seem as strong as the first time you smelt it. It is really but there is no need for your brain to keep reminding you. It is a bit like someone shouting at you to get your attention. Once you are listening, they talk to you in an ordinary voice.

Hearing

You might then hear the bubbling noises of the cooking. Sound is produced by vibrations which travel through the air. Your outer ear picks up the sound vibrations. These pass into the ear vibrating first the ear drum, then three tiny bones and finally some tiny hairs in a liquid filled tube which send messages to the brain via the auditory nerve. These hairs in your ears help you keep your balance. When you spin around, the liquid in your ears moves fast over the hairs which confuses your brain and makes you feel dizzy.

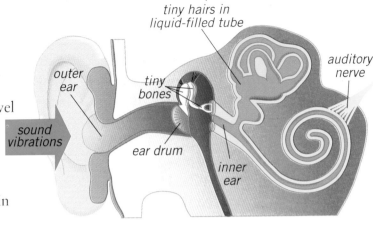

tiny hairs in liquid-filled tube

outer ear

tiny bones

auditory nerve

sound vibrations

ear drum

inner ear

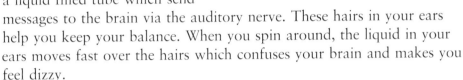

Seeing

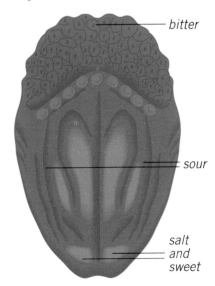

iris

retina

pupil

optic nerve

cornea

lens

When you are close to the pan you may see the steam rising. Your eye works by letting light in through the black centre (your pupils), then through a lens which makes the picture sharp. This picture lands on the back of the inside of the eye, called the retina. The optic nerve sends the picture on the retina back to the brain.

Touching

Getting close to the pan is dangerous. Your brain receives the heat signal from your skin. You feel the heat from the cooker. You are careful about the way you handle the pan. The skin on your hands is sensitive to touch. As you lift off the pan to pour out the food, all your senses and what you have learnt about hot things work together to make sure that you do not spill the hot food.

Tasting

Finally, when you eat the food, your senses of smell and taste are working. Your saliva or spit mixes with the food and helps spread the chemicals which give the food its taste over your tongue. Tastebuds on your tongue test the food for four main tastes – bitter, sweet, sour and salty. The messages are then passed from the tastebuds to the brain.

As we all need food and water to live, this is probably what made you become interested in the food in the beginning!

bitter

sour

salt and sweet

The nervous system

The human brain is connected to a spinal cord and then to a whole network of nerves. These nerves pass from the spinal cord through the whole body. This is the body's nervous system. The brain is the control unit which receives and sends messages through the nerves.

The messages are sent as tiny electrical currents which can pass along the nerves very fast. Fast enough to cover the length of a football pitch in one second! The brain contains 10 000 million nerve cells.

The brain does a whole range of different jobs. It keeps the body working all the time, and it supplies every part with food and oxygen. When changes happen outside, the brain makes sure the body reacts to the changes so no harm comes to it. Your brain will do things which can take you by surprise. For example, when you touch something hot you will pull your hand away without having to think about it. When this happens, your brain has avoided the normal nerve channels. This stops you from hurting yourself.

No control

There are other things that happen without you having any direct control. For example, when the light is bright, the pupil in your eye becomes smaller. This makes sure that light sensitive cells inside your eyes are not damaged.

This just happens and there is nothing you can do to control it. These things are controlled by the autonomic nervous system which keeps your heart beating and keeps you breathing, even when you are asleep at night.

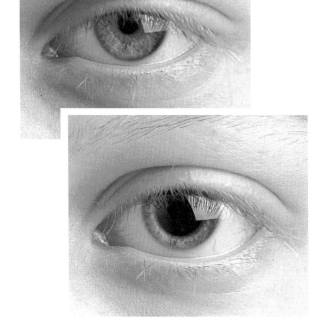

The pupil is small in bright light (above) and much bigger in dim light (below).

Thinking, hearing, speaking

Different parts of your brain control different things. Your brain is split up into three areas responsible for different aspects of your behaviour. These are the sensory cortex, the association areas and the motor cortex.

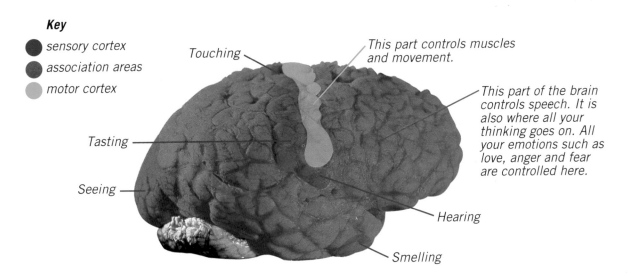

Key

● sensory cortex

● association areas

○ motor cortex

Touching

Tasting

Seeing

This part controls muscles and movement.

This part of the brain controls speech. It is also where all your thinking goes on. All your emotions such as love, anger and fear are controlled here.

Hearing

Smelling

The nerves

These messages are sent through the network of nerves, which are found all through your body. There are two main sorts of nerves. Sensory nerves work by taking messages (tiny electrical impulses) from the body through to the spinal cord and the brain. The brain makes sense of the message. If it needs to act, it sends a message back through different nerves (the motor nerves), to other parts of the body. All this happens very quickly and enables us to respond to the events going on around us.

What a nerve!

You can test some other things that your nervous system can do. Sit on a chair with one leg crossed over another. Use the edge of a ruler or book and tap just under your knee cap. The lower part of your leg will jerk up suddenly. This is known as a reflex action and it is your autonomic nervous system in control.

Skeletons and joints

The reason why your body does not flop all over the place is because there is a skeleton inside you. The bones do the same job as a clothes hanger does for a coat. Without the hanger, the coat is floppy. So the bones in a skeleton support and carry the weight of your body.

The 206 bones in a human body do two other jobs. They protect certain soft parts of the body. For example, the nerves which make up the spinal cord are all protected by many small bones. Together, these make up the backbone. The skull protects the brain, and the ribs protect the heart and the lungs. These parts of the body are very important for keeping you alive and so need extra special protection.

What is bone?

Bone is alive. It is made from strong bendy stuff called cartilage and a hard chalky chemical which gets added to the cartilage as you grow. The older you are, the more brittle the bone gets and the more easily it gets broken. There is still cartilage without any hard stuff in it – in your nose and ears. So the bone is a hollow tube which gives it extra strength. It is also strong yet light because of its honeycomb structure.

The centre of many bones is filled with a soft material called marrow. It is this part of the bone which is used to make new blood cells. There is also a layer of skin around the bone called the periosteum. This keeps the bone growing whilst it is young or when it needs to mend if it gets broken (see page 9).

air spaces make the bone light

hard bone gives the bone strength

periosteum (layer of skin)

in a living bone, bone marrow is found here

This is a cross-section of a femur (thigh bone).

Joints

The other thing bones allow you to do is move. Whenever two bones meet, they form a joint. Some joints move, others do not. The end of the joint is covered with protective cartilage. The two ends of the bones are joined together with straps called ligaments. These are attached to the bone and can move easily. The joint is covered with synovial fluid which acts like oil to keep the joints smooth. This helps the bone to move easily.

There are two main kinds of joints. The hinge joint which is in the elbows and knees, and the ball and socket joint which is in the shoulders and hips.

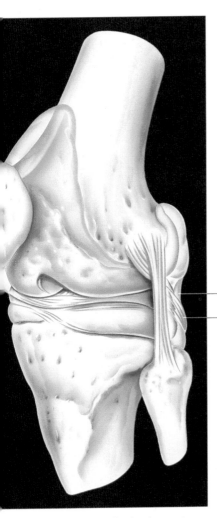

cartilage

ligaments

The knee joint is the largest joint in the body.

Broken bones

Bones can get broken. But because the bones inside us are living material, they can mend. This happens when the cracks in the broken bone grow over with new bone. The broken bone is held rigid in a plaster cast until it mends to make sure that the bone grows properly.

A broken bone in the upper arm (humerus) caused by sudden injury.

Muscles and movement

The skeleton supports the body but it is muscles which help to move the body. If you eat the meat from a cooked chicken or a lamb chop, or any cooked animal, you are eating the animal's muscle. So muscle is meat.

There are different types of muscle. The different jobs these muscles do means they are different in the way they are made up.

Muscles can only pull. None can push. There has to be two muscles to make your arm move. One to pull in one direction, the other to pull in the opposite direction. To bend your arm one muscle tenses, the other relaxes. To move it back to the first position, the relaxed muscle must now tense and the other one relaxes. Nearly all muscles have to work in this way. They work antagonistically. That simply means they work against each other.

Voluntary muscles

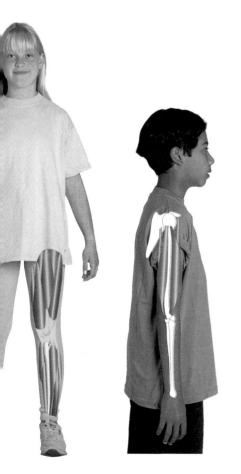

The big muscles in your body are those in your legs, buttocks and arms. They are known as skeletal muscles or voluntary muscles, because we decide when they work. For example, we know when we want to walk. So the muscle only works when we want it to.

Voluntary muscles are made up of bundles of overlapping tiny fibres. When you dangle your arm at your side, the muscle is at rest and the fibres are all relaxed. This makes the muscle long and thin. When you bend your forearm up, the muscle tenses. The overlapping fibres slide over each other and make a thick, fat, short muscle in the upper arm.

Involuntary muscles

When we swallow food, there are muscles working inside us to push the food down into the stomach. When the food is in the stomach, itself a muscular bag, it starts to twist and turn to churn up the food inside. These muscles are known as involuntary muscles because they work whether we like it or not. We have no control over them.

Heart muscles

Then there are the muscles in the heart. These are working every minute of the day, throughout your life, whether you are asleep or awake. The muscles in your heart have a structure that makes sure they never tire, which is just as well!

Fascinating fact

It takes 15 different muscles in our face to make a smile, and we use 200 muscles whenever we take a step!

Tendons

Muscles are joined to the bones they move by tendons. These tendons are flexible straps that pull the bones when the muscles contract. For example, there are no muscles in our fingers, only tendons. So when we move our fingers it is muscles in our arms which pull the tendons, which in turn pull the fingers into the positions we want.

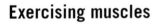

tendons

Exercising muscles

It is only exercise which keeps muscles healthy. Increase the amount of exercise and you increase the number of fibres in muscle. When a muscle stops working, for example, when an arm is in plaster, the muscle becomes weak because there are fewer fibres. The number of fibres increases as soon as the muscle starts being exercised again. It is important to have regular exercise to maintain your fitness (see pages 44–45).

How fast can a human body run?

The fastest male runners can finish the 100 metre sprint in under 10 seconds. That is a speed of 36 km per hour. The 100 metres is the fastest race, but the marathon is the longest at 42.2 km. The fastest runners in a marathon can travel at an average speed of 20 km per hour over this long distance.

A breath of fresh air

Breathing is something you do most of the time without having to think about it. The time you most notice it is when you are running and your body is making you breathe extra fast. The reason for breathing faster is that your body needs extra oxygen to keep going.

Oxygen is the gas that our bodies use to get the energy from the food we eat. Without oxygen or food, we would very soon die. So when we run fast or do a lot of exercise, we need even more of that oxygen than normal. Each time we get energy from our food we make waste materials, including a gas called carbon dioxide. So breathing is the way we bring oxygen into our bodies and get rid of the carbon dioxide which has built up inside us.

The lungs

You breathe by taking air into your body through your nose and mouth. The air travels down into a tube called a trachea which splits into two tubes called bronchi, one for each lung. Inside the lung, the bronchi split up into more and more smaller tubes called bronchioles. At the end of the bronchioles are tiny sacs called alveoli. Here, the blood vessels are so thin that oxygen from the air in the lungs can pass straight into the blood. At the same time, the carbon dioxide in the blood can pass directly out of the blood into the lungs. A huge area inside the lungs allows for all this swapping of gases to happen.

It is estimated that if the alveoli in a lung were flattened out, they would cover an area the size of a tennis court!

The lungs are made up of a mixture of tiny blood vessels and tubes for carrying air. They are rather soft and look spongy, but they are elastic too because they go up and down when you breathe.

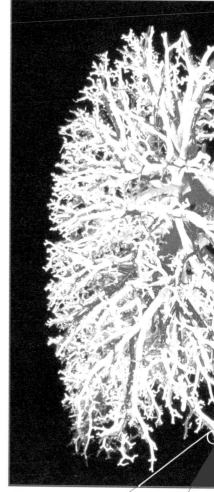

Air passages in the lungs

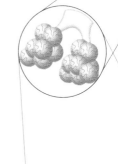

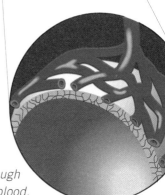

The alveoli. Oxygen passes through the blood vessels and into the blood.

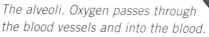

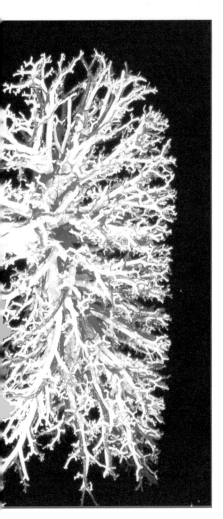

How do we breathe?

Your lungs lie in an airtight box formed by the ribs and the muscles which join them together, and a sheet of muscle called the diaphragm. There is a reason for the box to be airtight. As you breathe in, the muscles between the ribs push the ribs up and out. This causes the diaphragm to pull down and make the space in the box bigger (1). Air rushes into the lungs because of this extra space in the box. This makes them inflate like a pair of balloons, filling the extra space made in the airtight box with air. If the box was not airtight, this would not work. When you breathe out, the ribs move down and in and the diaphragm relaxes, pushing up into the box (2).

Both these movements reduce the amount of space in the box and the lungs get smaller, forcing air out through the mouth. Part of your brain controls this without you ever having to think about it (see page 7).

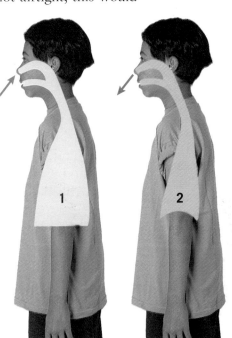

Breathe in, breathe out

Puffing trick

Here's a trick which will fool some people. Push a deflated balloon into an empty, plastic fizzy drink bottle. Make sure you stretch the open end of the balloon over the bottle's open mouth. Ask your friends to try and blow the balloon up. It is impossible because the bottle is filled with air. No matter how hard you blow into the balloon, the air in the bottle stops it from inflating.

Fascinating fact

What are hiccups? These happen when the muscle that controls your breathing (the diaphragm) moves suddenly and makes you gasp.

Heart and circulation

Inside your body is a system of tubes, called blood vessels, which carry blood around your body. There are three types of blood vessels: arteries, veins and capillaries. Blood in arteries carries food and oxygen to where it is needed. These arteries split up into smaller and smaller vessels called capillaries so that blood can get right into every part of our bodies.

These capillaries mix with the capillaries of other blood vessels called veins. This means that any waste materials such as carbon dioxide (a gas that we produce and need to get rid of) can be taken away by the blood in the veins. The veins then take the blood back into the heart.

Your heart is the pump that keeps the blood flowing around your body. The blood goes from your heart to your lungs before it goes anywhere else in your body. At the lungs, the blood gets rid of any carbon dioxide which can be breathed out. At the same time, the blood picks up oxygen and returns to the heart, ready for its journey around the rest of the body.

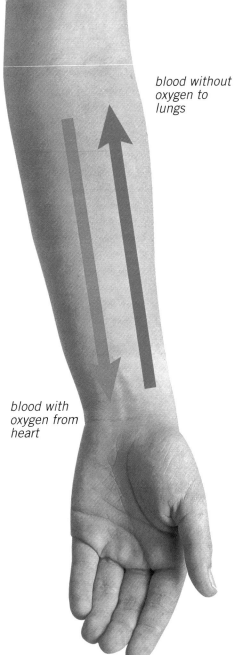

blood without oxygen to lungs

blood with oxygen from heart

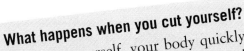

What happens when you cut yourself?

If you cut yourself, your body quickly starts to heal the wound. This happens when blood leaks out of the cut, cleaning the wound. The bleeding stops as soon as the platelets clot the blood which seals up the cut in your skin. This hardens and forms a scab and new skin grows underneath. The scab drops off and after a time you will not remember where the cut was.

How the heart works

To make all this happen, your heart beats 100 000 times each day and a healthy heart never gets tired. A heart is divided into two halves. Both halves each have chambers – an atrium at the top, and a ventricle below.

Blood enters the right atrium, is passed into the right ventricle and then off to the lungs. Blood returning from the lungs enters the left atrium, then the left ventricle and then off around the body.

Valves are found in the veins. These make sure that the blood keeps moving in one direction only. This avoids mixing up blood carrying carbon dioxide with blood carrying oxygen.

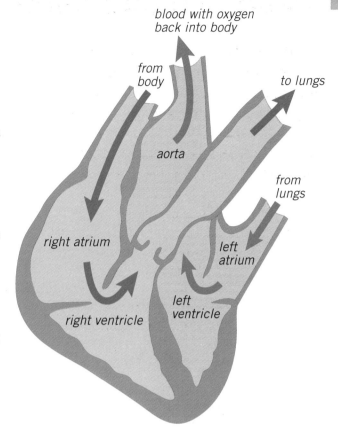

blood with oxygen
back into body

from
body

to lungs

aorta

from
lungs

right atrium

left
atrium

left
ventricle

right ventricle

What is blood made of?

Blood is made up of several different things. It is made up of plasma, red blood cells, white blood cells and platelets.

Most of your blood is plasma which is mainly water. Then there are the red blood cells. These carry oxygen around in the blood. To get oxygen, you need iron in your food which you can get from eating vegetables and red meat. There are about 200 million red blood cells in a drop of blood, but every minute you make

140 million new ones. The white blood cells eat bacteria and help fight off diseases. Finally, platelets cause the blood to clot and stop it leaking out when you cut or damage yourself (see page 14).

Other substances are mixed in with the blood. Food that you have eaten is turned into chemicals and dissolved into the water in the blood.

Red and white blood cells with platelets (blue)

Waste disposal

The very act of staying alive makes chemicals which are poisonous to us. When we breathe air, or when we eat anything, a chemical reaction takes place which keeps us alive. But at the same time, new chemicals are made that would kill us if we did not get rid of them. This is what the kidneys are for. They are the body's main filter system, taking out the waste material from the blood.

The process of removing poisons from the body is known as excretion. The kidneys are the main organs of excretion but there are other parts of the body which remove waste as well. These are the liver, the lungs and the sweat glands.

The kidneys

You have two kidneys, situated at either side of the bottom of your spine. They are the same shape as kidney beans, but they are much larger – about the size of your clenched fist.

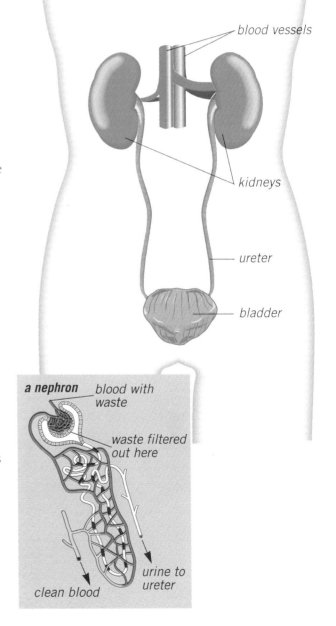

blood vessels

kidneys

ureter

bladder

The kidneys filter out the waste chemicals in the blood and remove any water the body does not need. The waste chemicals and the water are passed out of your body as urine. Kidneys are important as they keep the water balance of the body just right. For example, on hot days when you have lost a lot of water through sweating, there may not be much water in your urine. The urine will be dark yellow because there are a lot of waste chemicals and not much water.

Inside the kidneys are millions of tiny filtering units called nephrons that do the work. Unfiltered blood, containing waste material, is brought to the kidney in the renal artery and passes into the nephrons. It gets separated and clean blood is passed back into the body in the renal vein, and urine passes into the ureter.

a nephron blood with waste

waste filtered out here

clean blood

urine to ureter

The bladder

The ureters are long tubes which come out of the kidneys and pass into the bladder where urine is stored. When the bladder is full, it is ready to be emptied. This is what happens when we go to the toilet.

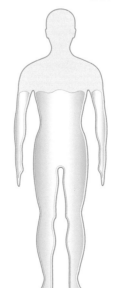

Losing water

Seventy per cent of our bodies is made up of water and we lose 3 litres of water each day.

There are three main ways of losing water: through the skin by sweating, through our breath when we breathe and by excretion in our urine. But the kidneys play an important role in making sure the salt and water balance in our bodies is right. This is done through hormones (see pages 26–27). These are special chemical messengers which are released into the blood when the water level is too low or too high.

Kidney machines

Some people have only one kidney. Others may suffer from kidney disease. These people have to have the poisons in their body removed by a special machine called a dialysis machine. Their blood supply is connected to the machine and it acts in the same way as a kidney. It filters out the poisons and puts clean blood back into the person's body. If the kidneys need replacing, it is even possible to transplant kidneys from one person to another.

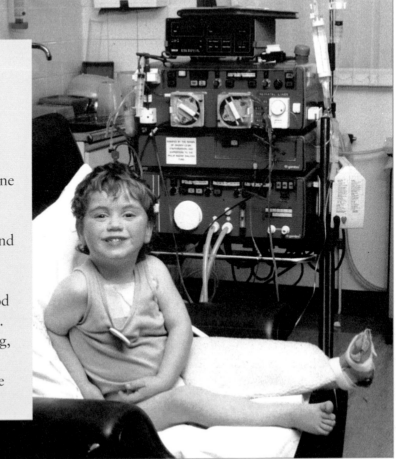

A day in your life

Your body goes through changes everyday. Whatever happens to you during each day, your body works hard to keep you well and comfortable. If you are healthy but become unwell, your body stands a chance of fighting any diseases. If you are unhealthy and unwell, then your body has a more difficult job to do.

Throughout each day, different things are happening in your body without you really noticing them. All these help to keep you feeling well.

Fast asleep

When you are asleep your heartbeat, breathing and body temperature level is low. You are using hardly any energy. All your muscles are relaxed. Your body is very still, so there is no need to for it to be working hard. That would be a waste of your body's energy.

Back at home

Now your body must recover by resting. You eat a meal and drink to boost your energy and fluid levels. You relax, your heartrate and breathing lower and your body is getting ready for rest. When you are in bed, your whole body slows right down. This gives your body a chance to make new cells to repair any damage to your body and fight infection.

Play sport

Playing sport will put your body through many changes. You will need a surge of energy to keep you running around on the games field. Heart rate and breathing will be high. Your body will be getting hot because of all the energy that you are using. Sweating takes the heat away from the body as it evaporates. As you play harder, you damage a part of your body. You don't notice at first. Your body deals with it by releasing adrenaline into your blood. Your lungs let in more air, and your heart pumps more blood to your muscles. Food stored in your liver is released to give more fuel to your muscles, and your skin turns pale because blood is sent from there to your muscles too. You sweat more too to keep the muscles cooled down.

Wake up!

When you first get up, your body has to make sure that your heartbeat, temperature and breathing rates all go up. For this to happen, your body needs more oxygen passing around it. You need to operate at the right temperature if all the chemical reactions going on in your body can take place. Your body is performing thousands of chemical experiments and these all happen best at a certain temperature – 37 degrees centigrade. You have a natural energy store from the food you ate the day before. This gives you the energy you need to get going. You also need to get rid of the waste that has built up in your body overnight, so you go to the toilet to empty your bladder.

Have breakfast

Breakfast is the first chance to get more energy into your body. You drink and eat food which is digested to give you the energy that you need to carry on through the day.

Walk to school

This is the first time today that your body is really using up energy. Your muscles need oxygen and they also need food. So your heart rate and your breathing rate both go up. You might be late and run some of the way, so you feel yourself sweating. Your body is losing some of the water that you drank at breakfast time to stop your body from overheating. When you get to school you will have to get a drink to replace the water your body has lost.

Sit in class

Now you are sitting still in class, both your heartbeat and your breathing rate have fallen. Your body needs less energy now because it is not moving around much. But as the morning goes on, you begin to feel hungry. This means you need more energy to keep your body temperature at a steady level. You go off to lunch and the level of sugar in your blood rises giving you energy. The hormone called insulin is produced to control the level of sugar in your blood and to make sure that just the right amount is released.

Nutrition and healthy eating

There is an expression, "You are what you eat." The food you eat contains the chemicals which will become part of your body. As you grow, particularly from a baby into a child, your body needs different foods to do different jobs.

For example, you need calcium to make bones grow. Eat the right kind of food and your body has every chance of being healthy. Eat the wrong kind of food and you could make yourself unhealthy, or even get diseases.

When people talk about eating a balanced diet, they mean eating a variety of different foods containing nutrients (see below). Make sure you eat a mix of foods to give you a balanced diet. Good food, such as fresh fruit and vegetables, helps to balance out food which is not so good for you, such as chips or chocolate. If you ate only the chips or chocolate, you would very quickly become unhealthy.

Energy

The food you eat has an energy value. On food packet labels it can be seen as kilojoules or kilocalories. So 100 grams of cereal is 1550 kj. A 100 grams of yoghurt is 220 kj. The first is very rich in energy, the second is less so. Different kinds of foods have different energy values. Food gives you the energy to stay alive and you depend on this.

Different kinds of people have different energy needs. A 12 to 14-year-old boy needs 11 000 kj, but a girl of the same age needs 9000 kj. If you spent your day running around, you would need more food than if you sat at a desk all day. But eating food isn't just about getting energy to live. Your body needs several different kinds of food, containing a variety of nutrients, if you are to stay healthy.

NUTRITION INFORMATION per 100g		
ENERGY	kj	1550
	kcal	370
PROTEIN	g	15
CARBOHYDRATE	g	75
(of which sugars)	g	(15)
(starch)	g	(60)
FAT	g	1.0
(of which saturates)	g	(0.5)
FIBRE	g	2.5
SODIUM	g	0.9
VITAMINS:		(% RDA)*
VITAMIN C	mg	100 (165)
VITAMIN D	mg	8.3 (165)
THIAMIN (B₁)	mg	2.3 (165)
RIBOFLAVIN (B₂)	mg	2.7 (165)
NIACIN	mg	30 (165)
VITAMIN B₆	mg	3.3 (165)
FOLIC ACID	mg	333 (165)
VITAMIN B₁₂	mg	1.7 (165)
IRON	mg	23.3 (165)

* Recommended Daily Allowance

NUTRITION INFORMATION
100 g provides
ENERGY 220 kj/52 kcal
PROTEIN 4.6 g
CARBOHYDRATE 7.3 g of which sugars 7.0 g
FAT 0.1 g of which saturates 0.1 g
FIBRE 0.1 g
SODIUM 0.1 g

Fibre

In a balanced diet, there needs to be a certain amount of fibre from plants. Vegetables, fruit, cereals and brown wholemeal bread all help to keep your digestive system healthy. They provide bulk which helps to move food along.

Carbohydrates

These are rich in energy and come mostly from plants. Bread, potatoes, pasta, rice, flour and sugar are high in energy. If you eat more of these than your body needs, your body will store what it does not need by converting it to fat.

Vitamins

These are found in different foods and you need thirteen different kinds to stay healthy. Vitamin A in carrots is good for your eyes and vitamin C in oranges helps to keep your gums healthy.

Protein

You need protein to keep your body growing and repairing itself, as well as for energy. Protein comes mainly from eating meat, fish, eggs and cheese, and also certain plants such as beans.

Fats

Energy-rich foods and fats are needed for growth of the nervous system and also new cell growth. Although we eat a lot of fat, found in butter, other dairy products and red meat, there is no real need to. Eating large amounts of animal fat can cause heart disease. Fats from plants are thought to be less of a health risk. These fats are in vegetable oils and margarine.

Minerals

These include salt (which you need in tiny amounts), calcium for bones and iron for blood. Calcium comes from milk and you can get iron from spinach.

Teeth

Without teeth, it would be very difficult to eat. You have two sets of teeth. You started to get the first set, your milk teeth, when you were about six months old. You probably lost these when you were about six. The second set gradually grew to replace your milk teeth. You can keep these for the rest of your life, if you look after them. Fortunately, we can go to the dentist if our teeth start to decay. But if you look after your teeth, they should last you a long time.

Some teeth in the second set often grow much later, when you are a teenager or even older. They are called wisdom teeth. Some people get all their wisdom teeth, while others get none.

Teeth grow from inside your jaw and have roots. These roots hold the tooth firmly in the jaw. Your teeth are different shapes and have different jobs to do.

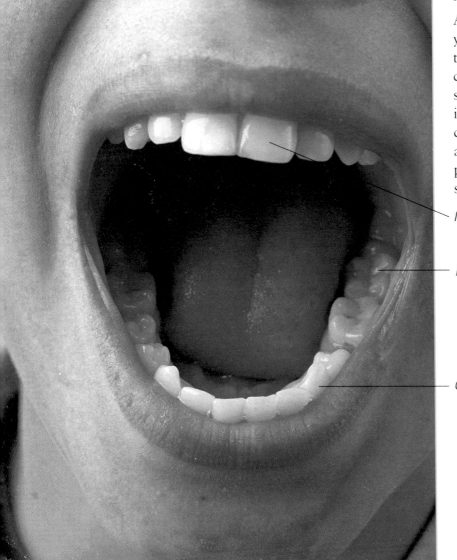

Incisor

Molar

Canine

Incisors and canines

At the front of your mouth you have incisors, and to the side of these you have canine teeth. Both have single cutting edges. The incisors are used for cutting food, the canines are used for tearing and piercing. They have a single root.

Premolars and molars

The teeth along your cheek at the back of your mouth are the premolars and the molars. They have a broad surface and are used for chewing and grinding up food. These teeth have two or more roots.

The photo (page 22) shows a molar tooth. The outside of the tooth (above the gum) is covered in a very hard substance called enamel. This is made of minerals – calcium and phosphorous. Most of the rest of the tooth, the part you cannot see because it is in your jaw, is made from hard dentine. Deep inside the tooth is an inner cavity with the pulp. This is the part of the tooth filled with nerves and blood vessels.

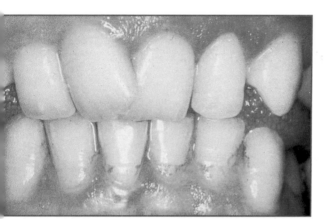

Healthy teeth

Some kinds of food are worse for your teeth than others. Cakes, sweets, biscuits, soft drinks, ice-cream, jam and anything with a lot of sugar in it will stick to your teeth and attract bacteria. This is because the sugar is food for the bacteria that live in your mouth. The bacteria use the sugar but make acid which then eats away at your teeth.

So to make sure you have healthy teeth, always brush them after a meal or eating sweet stuff. When you eat snacks, avoid eating sweets. Try to eat vegetables and fruit such as celery or apples, or even cheese, nuts or corn snacks.

A disclosure test uses red colouring to show plaque on the teeth.

Which teeth?

You can test the design of teeth by biting into an apple with your molars and then try chewing it with your incisors and canines. Also, when you are chewing, watch how your mouth moves. Is it up and down or side to side?

Fascinating fact

In 1979, a Belgian man, John "Hercules" Passis, the man with the strongest teeth in the world, kept a helicopter from taking off by using a mouth harness!

Chew it over

If you are hungry, then you will eat. Food gives you the energy and the chemicals your body needs to keep alive. But every piece of food must change before it can be useful to our bodies. It must be made smaller and smaller until it can be taken into the body.

Teeth and saliva

Teeth, together with saliva (or spit), begin this change. The incisor and the canine teeth cut, bite and tear up pieces of food. Then the molar and premolar teeth along the cheek at the back of the mouth crush and grind up the food (see page 23). Saliva contains a chemical called an enzyme which begins to break down some of the food. Chew a piece of bread and it quickly goes mushy. This happens because, besides grinding the bread with your teeth, there is a chemical reaction which is taking place in your mouth.

Digestion

When you swallow your food, it passes down your gullet or oesophagus (1) by a wave-like, muscular action called peristalsis. It enters your stomach (2) where it stays for about three hours. Your stomach twists and turns, and acid and digestive juices break down the food into a thick soup. Digestive juices made by the small intestine (3) and pancreas (4) turn the soup into chemicals small enough for them to pass into your body's blood supply. Small amounts of this soup enter the small intestine where more digestion happens.

The liver (5) produces a green liquid called bile which is stored in the gall bladder (6). Bile helps to break down fats. The wall of the small intestine is folded into millions of tiny 'finger shapes' called villi. This means that as much of the intestine as possible can be covered by the liquid food.

Tiny capillaries of blood lie in the wall of the small intestine and take the chemicals from the food. It is at this point that the food you eat really gets into your body. Up until then, it is just passing through your digestive system, never really becoming part of your body.

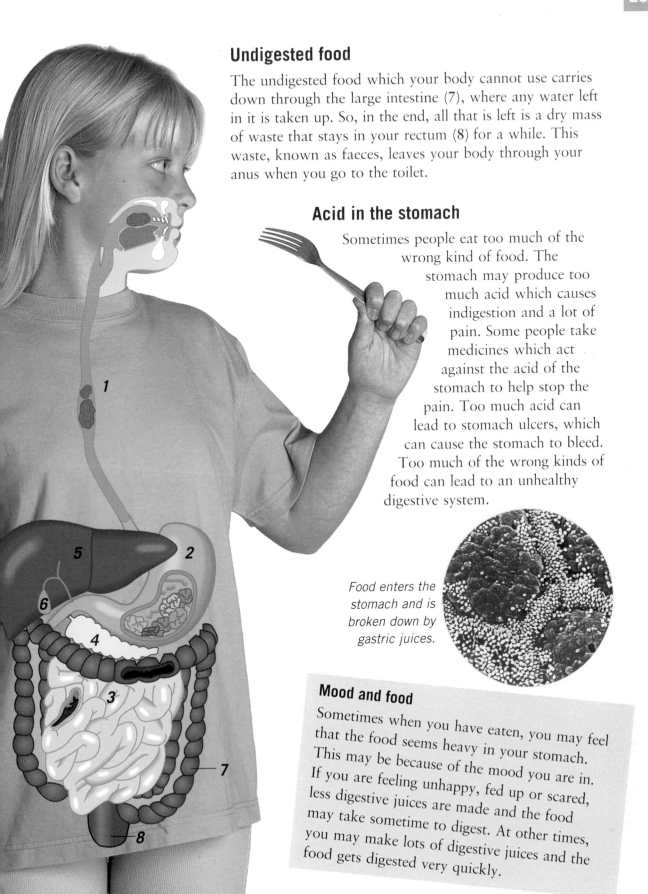

Undigested food

The undigested food which your body cannot use carries down through the large intestine (7), where any water left in it is taken up. So, in the end, all that is left is a dry mass of waste that stays in your rectum (8) for a while. This waste, known as faeces, leaves your body through your anus when you go to the toilet.

Acid in the stomach

Sometimes people eat too much of the wrong kind of food. The stomach may produce too much acid which causes indigestion and a lot of pain. Some people take medicines which act against the acid of the stomach to help stop the pain. Too much acid can lead to stomach ulcers, which can cause the stomach to bleed. Too much of the wrong kinds of food can lead to an unhealthy digestive system.

Food enters the stomach and is broken down by gastric juices.

Mood and food

Sometimes when you have eaten, you may feel that the food seems heavy in your stomach. This may be because of the mood you are in. If you are feeling unhappy, fed up or scared, less digestive juices are made and the food may take sometime to digest. At other times, you may make lots of digestive juices and the food gets digested very quickly.

Staying in balance

Each day of your life, your body is going through changes. Some changes happen quite quickly, such as when you feel hot after running around. Other changes are taking place over a much longer time, such as your growth. Some changes are almost immediate, such as when you are in an emergency and something horrible is about to happen. For example, when you fall off a bicycle, or when you wake up in a cold sweat after a nightmare.

All these things are controlled by tiny amounts of chemicals in your blood called hormones. Hormones are produced by special glands around your body. All these are controlled by the pituitary gland and a part of the brain called the hypothalamus. Hormones help your body get ready for changes whether they happen right away or over a long time.

Hormones are essential for our survival. They control so much in our bodies and they are very powerful because they can make instant changes as well as much longer changes.

Male hormones
The testes in a man make a hormone which helps control the development of male features such as a beard.

Female hormones
The ovaries in a woman make hormones which control both the development of female features when a girl grows into a woman and also a woman's periods and pregnancy.

The testes produce a hormone called testosterone which brings about the changes from boy to man at puberty (see page 34).

Hormones and glands

The **hypothalamus gland** (1) stimulates the pituitary gland to release hormones.

The **pituitary gland** (2) helps control the balance of water in your body by regulating the amount of water that is removed by your kidneys (see page 16). It also helps to control your growth and makes sure that a woman who has just had a baby makes milk to feed it.

The **thyroid glands** (3) control the way energy from food is released as well as controlling the temperature of your body. They also control the growth of your nervous system. The parathyroids, next to the thyroid glands, control the amount of calcium in your blood and bones.

The **pancreas** (4) makes an important hormone called insulin which controls the amount of sugar in your blood. Some people suffer from a disease called diabetes. This means their pancreas does not make insulin. Sometimes they have to inject themselves with insulin to keep the sugar in their blood at the right level.

The **stomach wall** (5) makes a hormone which turns on the production of acid in the stomach. The small intestine then releases another different hormone which turns the production of acid off. This means that acid is produced only when it is needed.

The **adrenal glands** (6) produce different hormones which help your body cope in an emergency. They also help with water balance, making sure that you have just the right amount of water in your body.

testes

Skin, nails and hair

Skin, hair and nails all have one thing in common. They are growing all the time. You have to cut hair and nails but as new skin grows the old, dead skin is just flaking off our bodies. Much of the dust around our home is caused by dead skin. A person one and a half metres tall gives off over 300 grammes of dead skin each year.

You can test for yourself that skin comes off. When you mark your hand with ink from a biro, it is difficult to get off. Watch how long it takes before it disappears. This is the time it takes for your skin to be replaced. Skin flaking off is the natural way for the germs and diseases which land on your body to be removed. But also, as you grow, new skin needs to be made. So your skin keeps growing and the old skin just flakes off all through your life.

What is skin?

Skin may look simple but a closer look shows that it is quite a complicated structure. The top layer is the epidermis, which is a dead layer of skin, that protects the body from infection. The layer beneath this is the dermis which is the living part of the skin. Here, there are hair follicles from which hair grows. Then there are oil glands to make the skin waterproof. There are sweat glands which produce sweat when our bodies get hot.

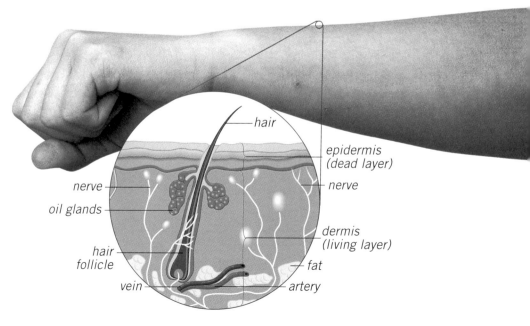

hair

epidermis (dead layer)

nerve

nerve

oil glands

dermis (living layer)

hair follicle

fat

vein

artery

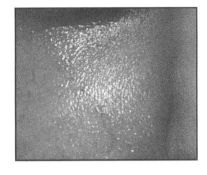

When we get hot, more blood vessels open up and blood flows closer to the skin so heat can escape. The hairs flop down and the sweat glands make sweat to help keep us cool. When we are cold, the blood vessels close down so heat cannot escape easily through our skin. At the same time, the hairs stick up and trap air between the skin and the cold air. This makes an insulating layer of warm air. If we were hairy all over, this would help us to stay warm. But because we do not have much hair, the empty hair follicles stand up on our skin and appear as goose pimples.

Sweat (above) helps us keep cool. Goose pimples appear when we are very cold.

Growing hair and nails

Hair and nails are made out of the same kind of stuff called keratin. Hairs grow, are shed, and then replaced by a new one growing underneath. Hair needs washing as the dried skin from our heads can create unpleasant dandruff.

Nails grow from skin that lies under the cuticle, the white half moon shape at the bottom of the nail. They grow all the time and need to be cut.

Caring for your skin

Although our body sheds skin to help keep clean, we need to wash regularly. Bacteria quickly grow on sweat and make it smelly. If we did not wash our skin, we would become very smelly, and not very popular with other people!

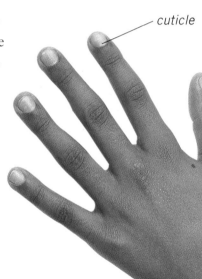

cuticle

Skin cancer

Skin can suffer from a disease called skin cancer. This can happen when your skin gets burnt by the sun. People with dark skin are at less risk than people with fair skin. This is because dark skinned people have more melanin in their skin than people with light coloured skin. Melanin is a pigment (substance) which protects skin from sunburn. To reduce the risk of getting skin cancer, it is a good idea to use high protection sun creams which stop skin from burning when you are in the sun.

Fighting diseases

Although skin can help to keep out germs that can cause disease, your body needs other, more powerful ways to deal with these invaders. This is because, from the day that you were born, all kinds of other living things get inside your body and can make you unwell. These include bacteria, viruses and even bigger living things called parasites. They are all around and our body has to fight them off.

Bacteria

Bacteria are everywhere, even living inside our digestive system. You can only see them through a microscope as they are so tiny. Some are harmful and if we swallow them, through eating bad food or drinking unsafe water or by cutting our skin, they get into the body. They spread very quickly and make us unwell. Bacteria cause diseases such as tonsilitis and some food poisoning. When a cut on your skin turns messy, you get yellow, sticky stuff around it called pus. That is caused by bacteria getting into the cut.

Viruses

Viruses are smaller than bacteria and they invade the living material in a cell, taking it over and using it to grow. Viruses can spread quickly through our bodies and cause diseases such as colds and flu, measles and chicken-pox. Many of the illnesses caused by both bacteria and viruses can be passed on to anothers through coughing and sneezing. When this happens, we say that the disease is infectious.

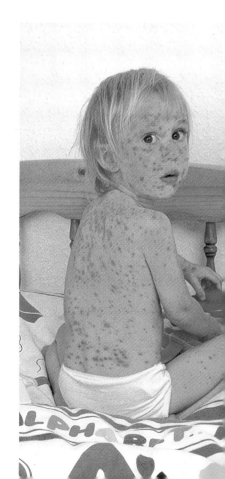

Chicken-pox is a mild infectious disease with an itchy rash and slight fever.

Antibodies

Your body fights infections and diseases through the lymphatic system. This is made up of vessels in your body connected to small swellings called lymph nodes. Special kinds of white blood cells, called lymphocytes, are made in these nodes. They make chemicals called antibodies which get into the blood when an invading germ enters your body. Each different germ causes a different antibody to be made. The antibody will help fight off the disease. When that germ appears again in your body, the antibody can be made very quickly. It can get rid of the germ much more easily, because it has made it once before. Knowing this has helped people to fight disease by using vaccination.

Vaccination

Vaccination works by injecting tiny amounts of dead or harmless germs into a healthy body, which will then make antibodies. Should the dangerous germs get into your body, the antibodies will be made very quickly. They will be able to defend the body and fight off the germs more easily. Being vaccinated helps you fight off the disease. Killer diseases such as polio and smallpox have been controlled through vaccinating people. Viruses are changing all the time and adapting to medicines. This means the human body will always have to fight off diseases.

Vaccination helps to reduce the risk of serious illness.

Wash hands

Hygiene

You can reduce the chances of getting diseases by making sure you wash your hands after going to the toilet, and before eating your food. Germs pass easily from the environment into your mouth so basic hygiene can help to make sure you do not get infected. People who handle food have to be particularly careful. They can easily pass on any infection they may carry to other people eating the food they have handled.

People are reminded to wash their hands, especially in food preparation areas.

Growing and changing

Even when you are asleep, your body keeps working all the time. It is also active in other ways, such as when you are growing. These changes take place most quickly when you are young. After birth, babies grow very quickly and they begin to explore, discover and find out about their environment.

As we grow, we experience and learn many different things which helps us survive. Eventually, we come to know about the world we live in. Not only does our knowledge grow, but we grow taller and the shape of our body changes as we grow.

Baby to child

A baby's face has a much smaller chin and nose than an adult, and very rounded cheeks and forehead. The baby's looks gradually disappear as a child grows.

Puberty

Between the ages of 10 and 14 years for a girl and 12 to 15 years for a boy, the next big change happens. This is called puberty where the body is getting ready to have children.

There is no right or wrong time for puberty. Everyone gets there in the end. Quite quickly, boys and girls begin the changes which will make them look and be more like adults. They can do things that adults can do but they still have to learn and experience different things about their bodies, themselves and the way they feel. They are no longer children. This new way of looking and being in the world means there are new things to learn about themselves and others who are growing around them.

Being an adult

At eighteen, they are an adult and their bodies are fully developed. Often this is the age when many people want to become more independent of their parents. They might even move away from home to take responsibility for their own life, without relying so heavily on their parents.

Growing older

The human body stops growing at around the age of twenty years. From that point on, our bodies are gradually slowing down. At about the age of fifty, the body begins to change again, although gradually. So the hair may become grey, muscles become weaker and the skin becomes looser and more wrinkled.

Women are not able to have babies any more because they no longer make the eggs they need to do so. From about the age of fifty, women begin a process called the menopause, when they stop having periods (see page 37).

When old age is reached, people may move more slowly, their bones become brittle and they are not so active. Yet these days, people are living longer than ever before. Many more are able to maintain a very active life at what used to be thought old age. Also, more people than before are now living to be a hundred years old.

Knowing your body – boys

As you grow, you will discover changes happening to your own body. These changes are completely normal and show you that you are becoming a man. Don't worry if they happen to you before or after other boys of your age. Nobody is exactly the same. This time of your life is known as puberty and here are some of the changes you will notice.

Changes to your body

Your voice will go croaky and sometimes sound strange. This is because your voice box is getting larger and your voice is 'breaking', making it sound deeper.

On your body you will see thick hair growing under your arms and wiry hair around your penis and testicles. The wiry hair growing around your penis is called pubic hair. You will also find hair growing on your face and you may also notice that you get spots too. Some people may have hair growing on their chest, legs and back. You may notice you are getting taller and your body is changing shape.

Ejaculation

Your penis grows but it also gets bigger and stiffer very quickly, particularly if you stroke or touch it. This is called getting an erection and happens because blood is pumped into the veins in your penis. When sticky, white liquid squirts out of your penis, this is called ejaculating. It may happen sometimes at night when you are asleep, and take you by surprise. This is known as a wet dream and happens because your body is still getting used to becoming an adult. The white sticky liquid is called semen. It contains seminal fluid and the sperm which you need to help a woman make a baby.

Male sex organs

The picture shows a penis and a pair of testicles. The penis is covered with a foreskin. When a penis is erect, the foreskin is pushed back to show the glans which feels sensitive to the touch. Some people have the foreskin removed for religious or health reasons. White creamy stuff called smegma is made under the foreskin and this helps it move more easily over the glans. When you have passed puberty, it is important to regularly wash stale smegma off your glans.

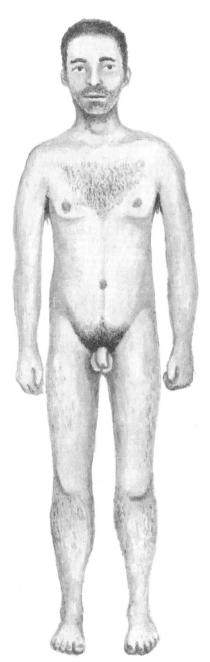

The testicles are made up of the scrotum (the loose bag of skin which holds two testes). The testes make the sperm, and the sperm pass along tubes which join the urethra (see page 38). Urine passes down this tube, as well as semen, but the two never mix. In each ejaculation there is about a teaspoonful of semen which contains around 300 million sperm.

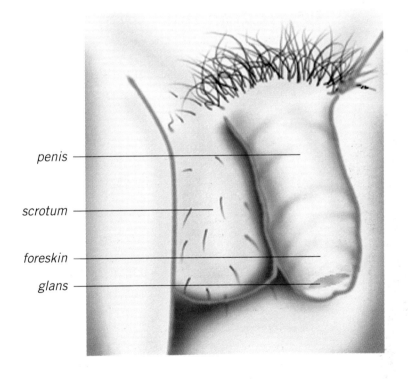

penis

scrotum

foreskin

glans

Knowing your body – girls

From about the age of ten to eighteen, girls will go through some very big changes in their bodies. This time of change is known as puberty. It is your body getting itself ready to have babies. For some, the changes happen early; for others, much later. It really does not matter at what time these changes happen, but they will always happen eventually.

Changes to your body

You may first notice thick hair growing under your arms, and wiry hair growing around your vagina area. This wiry hair is called pubic hair. Your breasts begin to grow bigger and become special glands. After having a baby, these glands will make milk to feed the baby. Your hips grow wider so that a baby has room to grow inside the womb. You will start to bleed from the vagina. When this happens it is called having a period.

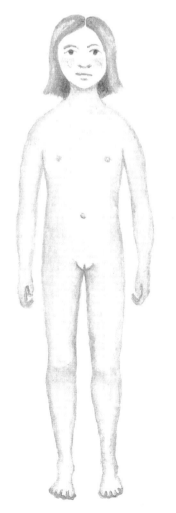
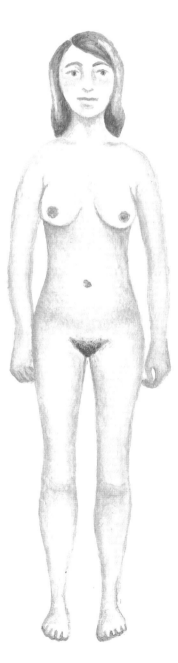

Periods

When you start to have periods they may not be regular. After a time, they will happen once every 20 to 36 days and will last from two to six days. A period is the first few days of the menstrual cycle. About fourteen days after the period starts, an egg is released by an ovary (**1**) and passes down a fallopian tube (see page 38). Meanwhile, the lining of the uterus (the womb) has become filled with blood and ready to receive a fertilized egg (**2**). (A fertilized egg is an egg which has joined with a sperm.) If the egg is unfertilized, the uterus lining and the blood come away and pass out through the vagina. This is a period (**3**).

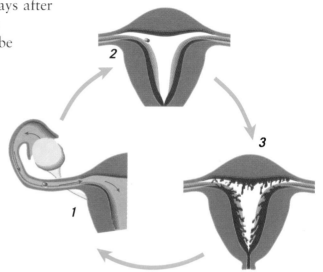

Female sex organs

The picture shows the female sex organs between your legs. The vagina is part of these organs. It is the way out for the blood from a period. It is also where a baby comes out. It is where a man's penis fits, and the way in for sperm to reach an egg. Across part of the opening to the vagina is a thin layer of skin called the hymen. This may break as you grow, or it is harmlessly broken during first sexual intercourse.

Above the vagina is the urinary opening which is connected to your bladder. This is where urine comes out. Above this is the clitoris which is sensitive to touch and helps to make you feel good during sex. Two pairs of skin flaps cover all of these openings. On the outside are the thicker, outer labia or 'lips'. These protect the inner labia underneath. The inner lips are more sensitive. All these structures together make up the vulva.

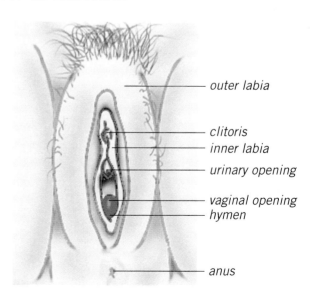

outer labia

clitoris
inner labia

urinary opening

vaginal opening
hymen

anus

Sex and reproduction

Sex is something most animal life has to do to make more of their own kind. In other words, to have babies. It happens when a sperm meets an egg. For human beings, the sperm has to get from the man's testicles into the woman's vagina, near the neck of the womb (uterus). This happens during sexual intercourse.

During sexual intercourse, the man and the woman want to be very close. Being close in this way is exciting for both. The man's penis becomes erect, and the woman's vagina gets larger and slippery. When they are both ready, the man puts his penis inside the woman's vagina. Both the man and the woman enjoy sexual intercourse because often they each experience something known as an orgasm. An orgasm makes them feel good all over. The woman gets her orgasm through her clitoris, and the man through his penis when he ejaculates (releases sperm).

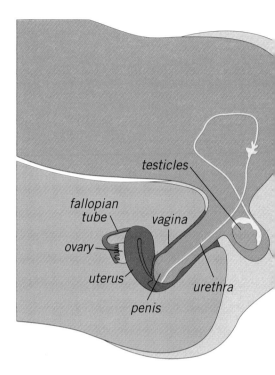

The sperm and the egg

Once inside the vagina, around 300 million sperm begin to swim up into the uterus to find the egg. Each sperm has a head and a tail, and it swims by using its tail. A few hundred sperm cells will reach the egg which is in the fallopian tube, but only one will fertilize the egg to start a new human being. The fertilized egg then passes down the fallopian tube, ready to attach itself to the uterus wall.

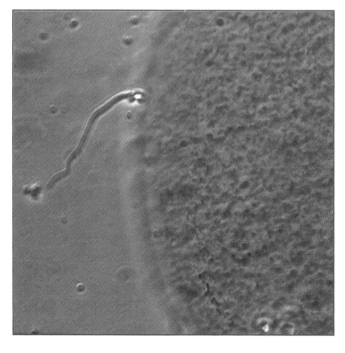

Once a sperm has penetrated the egg wall, no other sperm can reach the egg.

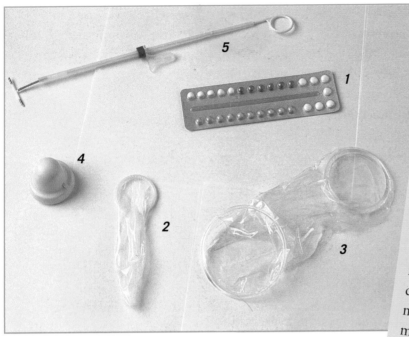

Disease

It is possible for one person to pass on diseases to another as a result of sexual intercourse. These are called Sexually Transmitted Diseases and most can be treated by a doctor. Some diseases, such as AIDS, cannot be cured. When a man uses a condom, it lowers the risk of passing on any disease. Using a condom makes sexual intercourse much safer.

Contraception

Some people have sexual intercourse even though they do not want to have babies. So they may use different ways to stop them from having babies. This is called contraception. Not everybody wants to use contraception because of religious or other reasons. There are several different kinds of contraceptive including:

The pill (1) – a chemical contraceptive taken by women that stops them making any eggs. When the man's sperm get inside her, there are no eggs there for them to fertilize.

The condom or sheath (2) – used mostly by men. This is a barrier contraceptive, because it acts as a barrier to the sperm. The man slides it over his penis, and the sperm are caught inside the condom, never going into the woman at all. There is also a female condom which is inserted just inside the woman's vagina (3).

The cap (4) – another barrier contraceptive used by the woman. She puts it inside her at the top of the vagina on the neck of the womb (the cervix). It blocks the path of the sperm even though they are in the vagina. The cap is covered with spermicide cream, a chemical that kills sperm which slip through.

The coil (5) – has to be fitted by a doctor and it stays at the top of a woman's vagina. Nobody is quite sure how the coil stops women from becoming pregnant.

All contraceptives work by stopping the sperm and the egg meeting.

Choosing a contraceptive that suits a man and woman needs thought. Some methods are better at stopping babies, such as the pill, but because chemicals are being put into the woman's body there are some risks to her health.

Pregnancy and having a baby

When an egg has been fertilized by a sperm, it is ready to attach itself to the inside of the uterus or womb. Each month, since puberty, the uterus has been prepared for this moment. Whilst the new life is growing, the uterus lining will stay in place and help it to develop. The woman will have no more periods whilst the new life grows inside, because the uterus lining stays in place to help the fertilized egg develop.

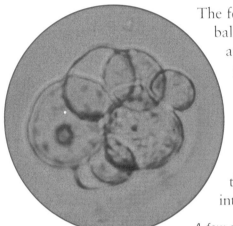

The fertilised egg will divide and divide again, forming a ball of cells. This ball will eventually grow into the baby, and is fixed to the uterus where the placenta grows. The placenta is important to the baby because it is the link between the baby's blood and the mother's blood. The baby's blood and the mother's blood don't mix: they simply exchange things. The baby is connected to the placenta through its umbilical cord and all the mother's food and oxygen passes into the baby along this cord. All the waste that a baby makes passes back into the mother's blood supply through it too.

A few days after conception and the new life is a ball of cells.

The baby is surrounded by a special sac filled with a liquid called amniotic fluid. This helps to cushion the baby from bumps and sudden movements. The baby remains here for up to nine months growing inside the mother. As it grows, it goes through big changes.

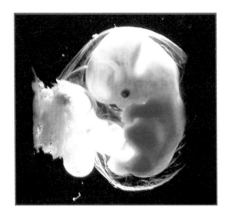

Six weeks pregnant. The baby's heart starts to beat for the first time. All internal organs have begun to form.

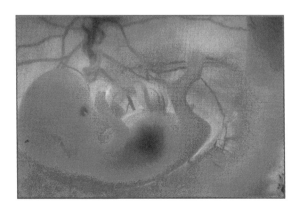

By 12 weeks all the baby's brain, heart and other organs have formed. It weighs 18 grams and is about 6.5 cm long.

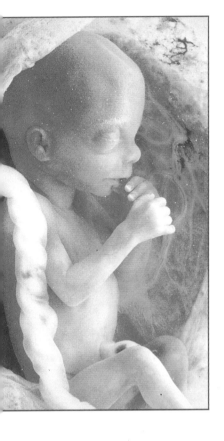

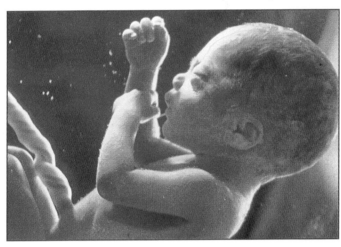

At 26 weeks, the baby has been moving around and the mother regularly feels the baby kicking. It is 30 cm long.

At around 40 weeks, the baby is ready to be born.

Being born

Shortly before birth, the neck of the womb or cervix slowly opens up and the walls of the womb push the baby down out through the mother's vagina. When the baby comes out, it takes its first breath and cries. It is still connected to the inside of the mother through its umbilical cord. This is cut and tied off. Our tummy button is the scar that is left after we have had our umbilical cord cut. The placenta comes out of the mother a little later after the baby, and so it is often called the afterbirth.

The mother is ready to feed the baby as her breasts begin to make milk for the baby to feed on.

At the first feed, the mother's antibodies, which help to fight disease, are passed to the baby.

Taking responsibility

Part of growing up is thinking for yourself and working out how you want to do things. As you grow older, your parents realise that you no longer want to be told what to do and how to do it. They will give you more freedom to choose for yourself. And you will want to do things your own way.

But with this greater freedom comes a greater sense of responsibility. If you do things your way and they go wrong, you will have to take the blame! Everyone has to learn by making mistakes, even adults. That is just part of learning.

When you are young, you will probably make more mistakes than when you are older. As you grow up, you will realise that only one person can take responsibility for your body and keeping it healthy – you! Only you can know what you are putting into your body and whether it will do you harm. Even if you do something because everyone else is doing it, this does not make it right.

So caring for your body is your responsibility. Here are some things you need to be responsible about. Your body depends on it.

Alcohol

You need to know that alcohol is a drug. Like any drug, it can change the way you feel and can change the way you behave. Quite small amounts can slow down your reactions. When people drink alcohol and then drive a car or other vehicle, they risk their own lives and the lives of others. This is because they are unable to properly judge what is happening around them. Also, many people become violent and may hurt others for no reason. Every day, people are hurt or killed because someone has drunk too much alcohol. Too much alcohol can also lead to kidney and liver failure.

'Drink and drive' warnings

Smoking

Cigarettes, cigars and pipe tobacco contain a drug called nicotine, together with lots of other chemicals. They can cause a disease called cancer. They also cause the lungs to slow down the way they work and the lungs become full of dirt and tar. Smoking cigarettes also increases your chances of getting lung and heart diseases. Most people now agree that smoking is very unhealthy.

A healthy lung

This lung shows patches of tar caused by cigarette smoke.

Drugs

These include marijuana, tablets such as ecstasy and LSD, and hard drugs such as heroin and cocaine. All these drugs change the way people behave. Some, such as the hard drugs, are very addictive and some people turn into addicts. These are people who need to take drugs just to be able to live their life. They find it very difficult to give up because their body has become so used to having the drug. Taking drugs is very dangerous to the health of your mind and body.

All these substances in some form or another are poisons in your body. Your body has to battle against these chemicals each time they enter it. Only you can be responsible for the health of your body.

Exercise

Exercise is particularly important these days. A lot of people spend longer resting than being active. We sit in front of computers or watch television, or even just watch others play sport without playing any ourselves. Taking regular exercise tones the body and helps to keep it healthy.

Exercise helps your body in the following ways:

 It builds up your stamina which means you can do all the other things in your life better and more easily. Even getting down to doing your homework can be improved by having a good level of stamina!

 It makes your heart stronger which gets your circulation working well. Good circulation means that oxygen gets to all the parts of your body.

 It makes your lung capacity bigger which means you can breathe in more oxygen and get rid of carbon dioxide more efficiently.

 It helps to keep your weight down because your body uses up more energy and stores less of the food you eat as fat.

Strength test

Take some ordinary bathroom scales and squeeze them as hard as you can. Make a note of the reading. By exercising your arms and hands, you may be able to make your grip stronger. Using the same scales, test your leg strength. Ask someone to hold the scales against the wall and then, lying on your back, you press your feet against the scales as hard as you can. The person holding the scales can take the reading for you.

It stimulates your brain to make natural body drugs. Some of these are called endorphins and they leave you with a sense of feeling good and feeling happy.

It strengthens your muscles so you are able to do all kinds of tasks more easily. It strengthens your joints and makes the muscles in your body supple.

Safety warning

Anyone who hasn't exercised for a while should start gently and gradually build up the level of exercise.

So exercise is important for everyone's health. Whilst at school, periods of strenuous exercise through playing games will help. It is now recommended that you need five 30 minute sessions of exercise a week. Playing sports such as tennis, running, going swimming or cycling all help to keep your body working at peak performance. You do not have to do sport every day, but getting into a habit of doing some strenuous exercise is a good way of making sure that you stay healthy.

Health test

You can test your fitness by measuring your pulse rate before and after taking exercise. To find your pulse rate, feel your pulse for 30 seconds, then double the number. Take your pulse at rest. Then take exercise such as stepping up and down on a step for a couple of minutes. Now take your pulse again. See how long it takes to get back to your resting level. This is a rough measure of how fit you are. The quicker you take to get back to your resting pulse rate, the fitter you are.

Staying healthy

To get the most out of your body, you have to treat it right. If you eat fatty or sweet foods all the time, smoke cigarettes, drink a lot of alcohol, take drugs, go to bed very late and never take any exercise, your body will soon tell you it is unhappy. You will feel unwell a lot of the time, and you will find it difficult to enjoy life to the full. You will have more chances of getting a disease, or even dying at an early age.

A good diet

You need a balanced diet. Protein in meat, fish and eggs helps you grow. Avoid too many fatty foods such as crisps, and sweet foods such as cakes and sweets. Try to eat as much fresh vegetables and fruit as you can. They not only give you the fibre to avoid constipation, but also the vitamins you need to help ward off everyday infections and diseases such as colds.

Regular exercise

When you are at school, you will probably do some kind of sport. Strenuous exercise is good because it makes your heart beat faster, makes you breathe deeper and allows your muscles to become stronger. It also keeps your body supple, not stiff. Without exercise, your muscles really do waste away (see pages 44–45).

Sleep

This is your body's time to recover. All the experiences of the day are sorted out in your brain and stored there for the future. Your dreams are part of this process. When you are asleep, your body will be able to fight off infections and repair itself. This is because many of the other body functions have slowed down, allowing your body to concentrate on this rather than anything else. You will need between six and nine hours sleep each night, and you need more sleep when you are young.

Washing

It is essential that you keep your body clean. Dirt on the body attracts bacteria which can cause diseases and infections. Washing yourself regularly reduces the chances of you getting diseases. When you reach puberty, your skin becomes much greasier so you may need to wash more to avoid too many spots. Do not forget to clean your teeth regularly, at least twice a day. Use dental floss to get rid of plague and waste food which can get stuck between your teeth.

Remember – take care of your body!

Published by BBC Educational Publishing, a division of BBC Education

First published 1996

© Steve Pollock/BBC Worldwide (through BBC Education) 1996

The moral right of the author has been asserted.

Paperback: 0 563 37504 3

Hardback: 0 563 37556 6

Colour reproduction by DOT, England

Cover origination by Sonicon Ltd, England

Printed and bound by Cambus Litho Ltd, Scotland

Illustrations: © Salvatore Tomaselli 1996 (pages 2–6, 8, 10–12, 14–17, 24–28, 30, 34–38 and 40), © Claire Bushe 1996 (pages 18, 19, and 34–36)

Photos: Ardea/P. Morris **p. 8 (right)**; BBC/Luke Finn **p. 39 (left)**; BBC/Lesley Howling **p. 29 (top and bottom)**, **32 (middle right)**; Gibbs Oral Hygiene **p. 23 (top and bottom)**; Robert Harding Picture Library/Delimage **p. 41 (bottom)**; Image Bank/Steve Allen **p. 41 (top left)**; Courtesy of the Kidney Foundation, Midlands **p. 17**; Published by the Portman Group **p. 42 (middle and right)**; Rex Features London **p. 43 (bottom)**; Science Photo Library/Alex Bartel **p. 30 (bottom)**; Science Photo Library/John Bavosi **p. 9 (left)**; Science Photo Library/CNRI **p. 25 (right)**; Science Photo Library/Ken Eward **p. 15**; Science Photo Library/Matt Meadows/Peter Arnold Inc. **p. 9 (right)**; Science Photo Library/Petit Format/JD Bauple **p. 7 (top)**; Science Photo Library/Petit Format/CSI **p. 40 (top)**; Science Photo Library/Petit Format/Nestle **pp. 40 (bottom)**, **40 (middle right)**, **41 (top right)**; Science Photo Library/Richard Rawlins **p. 38 (right)**; Science Photo Library/Jim Selby **p. 31**; Science Photo Library/James Steveson **p. 43 (top left and right)**; Telegraph Colour Library **p. 33 (left)**; Telegraph Colour Library **p. 32 (far left)**; Wellcome Institute Library, London **pp. 12–13**; Zefa Pictures UK **pp. 32 (middle left)**, **33 (middle)**, **33 (right)**

All other photographs: BBC/Simon Pugh

Front cover: Stockfile/Steven Behr **(main)**; Science Photo Library/Custom Medical Stock Photo **(inset)**

Grateful thanks to Jane Goodman and Eastman Dental Hospital, London